FOCUS

A 30-DAY DEVOTIONAL
TO ENCOURAGE YOUR LIFE

Mike Sternad

FOCUS
A 30-DAY DEVOTIONAL TO ENCOURAGE YOUR LIFE

BY MIKE STERNAD

Mailing Address: 312 T Schillinger Rd. S, Mobile, Alabama 36608
Website: www.calvarychapelmobile.com
Email: mikesternad@gmail.com

Published by Contented Life Publishing
Printed in the United States of America

Edited by Miriam Rogers
Cover Design by Ashley Garcia
Interior Design by Ulrika Towgood

This book is dedicated to
the saints at Calvary Chapel Mobile.
Thank you for your love and support;
for coming alongside my family and me
through the years. God is on the move
and we're just along for the ride!

TABLE OF CONTENTS

TABLE OF CONTENTS

FOREWORD

Most writers ask someone to write the foreword to lend credibility to their book. Normally, they would ask a better-known writer, someone with more mileage on their tires or with some street cred to say, "Hey man, check this book out. It's legit!" But Mike didn't do that. Instead, he asked me. Here's why—Mike doesn't deal in the world's economy. He isn't overly concerned with celebrity endorsement or flash. I've seen his church! He's a couple of years into a church plant and still doesn't have a laser light show or fog machine! The most impressive aspect of Calvary Chapel Mobile is their simplicity of heart and focus on keeping Christ the center. They keep the main thing the main thing.

Mike and I share a common experience of church planting in the Deep South, and after the many conversations that we've had, one thought he has shared with me stands out as the drumbeat holding the entirety of his ministry together: "I'm just along for the ride." He clings to the Person of Jesus Christ for dear life as our Lord leads him down this well-weathered path of servitude, heartache, sanctification, and joy. I get to watch these things from three hours away. He may not even know we're watching, but we are. Even as I give thanks to the Lord for the work that He is doing with Mike, his wife Brianne, and their children, I also find that I am convicted by his faith, focus, and drive.

A hallmark of Mike's indelible drive is how he burns the candle at both ends, in the best sense. He is one of those people that, by the grace of God, will have left nothing on the field when the Lord takes him home. He is intensely focused on serving God and serving God's people. To this end, Mike knows something about focus. He has willingly and purposefully set his mind on things above, not on things of the earth, so that He might please Jesus in his every act of worship.

This book is one of those acts of worship. *Focus* lifts Jesus higher. It helps us, distracted wanderers, to do the same. So often we are beat down by our circumstances. Or more likely, we subvert our own focus by willfully disobeying God's Word. Mike equips us by simple, gracious and practical encouragement that we can meditate on and exercise daily.

Focus, dear one. Set your mind on things above.

Anthony Rea
Pastor, Living Water Christian Fellowship
Dothan, Alabama

INTRODUCTION

It was foggy and cold one night and my wife was driving with some friends to a certain destination. She started to drive before the windshield was completely defrosted, her head tilted downward as she peered through the only portion of the windshield she could see through. Her friends were terrified wondering if they'd make it to their destination alive! When my wife was telling me this story, we were laughing; we thought it was a hilarious scene! But at the moment her passengers were filled with fear as they watched Brianne go seventy miles per hour, not seeing the road clearly. To focus means to have the quality of clear vision, to concentrate and to look to a fixed point. The panic would have been lessened if the windshield was clear and conditions were favorable.

Oftentimes, life can be blurry and unclear. Certain situations can cause distraction and lure us away toward things that do not matter. Lack of focus really has become an epidemic in our society and our world today! When it comes to the focal point of our lives, I believe the Lord should be the fixed point to which our eyes and hearts should constantly be aimed. We look to God through prayer, through connection with other believers, and through His Word. When the things of God become our focus, then our faith will increase and become more activated. Focusing on the Word of God can annihilate anxiety, defeat depression and sink sadness. This is the point of this devotional—*Focus.*

We all need encouragement and the best source of encouragement comes from consistently getting into the Scriptures. Before I even began walking with God I was reading the gospel of Matthew. I had deep questions about life and I wanted to know the answers! As I read, I quickly realized that the Bible is not a philosophy book full of questions to ponder, it's a book that is full of answers! Once I started reading the Bible, I was hooked! As I focused on the Scriptures, my desires began to radically change. The Word of God transformed my life—it turned a drugged-out, hippy-wannabe, institutionalized kid into a child of God. The Lord began to refine my life and show me the way to true fulfillment and total rest. The more I focused on reading truths from the Bible, the more I learned, and the more I learned, the more passionate I became to live fully for God.

My motive in writing this devotional is to help people foster a spiritual habit of getting into God's Word on a regular basis. We are always capable of growing and going deeper with the Lord. One page, one paragraph, even one word from the Word of God can lift up a person's countenance like nothing else can. We need to extract our encouragement from the love letter that God has written to humanity. I believe my mission in life is to get God's Word out and to help people consistently dig into the Word of God. We will hunger and have an appetite for what we constantly feed off of. I used to hate sushi, until I tried it. The idea of raw fish grossed me out until my friend whom I lived with in Venice Beach, who graduated from Sushi Academy, talked me into trying it. Wow. It was so good. My appetite for sushi grew to such an extent I had regular cravings for it! Spicy tuna rolls, please! The same goes with God's Word. The more we get into it, the more we grow, and the more we hunger and thirst for it.

Your focus will determine your faithfulness. If you are focused on the carnal actions of the world, you will desire to stay in the middle of that mess. If you are focused on Jesus and the things of God, you will be in the middle of your divine mission. The Lord has given you free will to decide who, what and where your eyes are to focus. My prayer is that this devotional will keep your eyes looking up and your heart bent toward the Lord. Focus on Jesus. It's all worth it.

Mike Sternad
Pastor, Calvary Chapel Mobile
Mobile, Alabama

DAY 1

NEW MERCIES

Through the LORD's mercies we are not consumed, because His compassions fail not. They are new every morning; great is Your faithfulness. (Lamentations 3:22-23)

Do not condemn yourself or beat yourself up. Instead, marvel at God's mercy and stand in awe of God's comforting compassion. How astounding to know that you deserve the worst because you are innately sinful, yet God holds back the darkness and shines His light into your life because He loves you. That's mercy!

Within each of us is an innate instinct to condemn ourselves for what we have done apart from the Lord. We're often harder on ourselves than God is on us! Self-condemnation can crush our countenance and engulf us in major guilt and shame. But we are not called to beat ourselves up for something that God has forgiven us for. It's time to accept that God is a forgiver toward those who've come clean with Him. People mistakenly view God as a tyrant who is waiting for His creation to commit the smallest sin, so He can hammer down the gavel of judgment. God is not an evil King who constantly says things like, "Off with his head!"

This is far from God's heart. God absolutely loves

you and wants you to know that when you repent, the result is true forgiveness!

We are not called to beat ourselves up for something that God has forgiven us for.

God's mercy is ready and waiting for you to receive it. *Mercy* means that God doesn't give us what we deserve. As sinners we were born with a heart that is bad and tendencies that are carnal. When we began walking with Jesus, we were saved, sealed and set apart to live for Him! Therefore, we can live guilt-free because He took our place on the cross so that our sins could be forgiven. We are free from darkness, death and destruction. Last night is over and today Your Maker is giving you new mercies. One definition of *mercy* is "goodness and kindness." God is so good and kind that He blesses us even though we don't deserve anything good! We can praise God today because He has every reason to take us out but chooses not to. The Lord loves us too much to not lavish us with His mercy. May we stand in awe at the heart of God in giving us daily mercies.

Open your heart and receive mercy and compassion from the Lord. He is not a condemner; He is a forgiver. Rest in that truth and revel in that reality. God's mercy does not last for a moment, it lasts all day long, every day of our lives. Don't forget that the Lord loves you too much to leave you stuck in the rut of guilt. If you are walking with the Lord, live in freedom and forgiveness. He is faithful to forgive you now and forever.

DAY 2

HEART PEACE

Peace I leave with you, My peace I give to you; not as the world gives do I give to you. Let not your heart be troubled, neither let it be afraid. (John 14:27)

Peace is hard to find and impossible to conjure. In this crazy and chaotic world that we live in, peace is certainly a precious commodity. As you look into the Word of God, you can see clearly that having peace is actually a possibility. The truth is that the source of peace is the Savior of the world.

The first step to having peace in your heart and your life is to realize that Jesus is the peace giver. The next step is to receive His peace. If you are searching for peace from a person, an occupation, or material items, your search will last the rest of your life with absolutely no results. We try so hard to pretend like we are fulfilled with the junk that we accumulate. The more material items we have, the more secure we would feel, right? Wrong. *Maybe a relationship will solve all the turmoil that has accumulated in my mind.* Nope. *Surely a long vacation at an exotic resort on the beach will finally calm my heart and give me rest.* Think again. The source of peace is not a place; it's a Person—Jesus. The fountainhead of rest is not a vacation; it's the Victor—Jesus. The giver of solace is not a beach scene; it's the Savior—Jesus. May we be reminded today that the source of serenity

15

is not found on this earth, it is found when we focus on the eternal and spiritual things in life!

When it comes to true heart peace, the bottom line is that this world has nothing to offer!

When you listen to the words of Jesus, you come to realize He is the possessor and giver of peace. Before I was a Christian I would search high and low for peace and some kind of rest and solace. I read books, took actions and followed trends that promised true peace and real happiness. Guess what? It was all a lie! Nothing worked! The only time in my life where I had peace that was palpable and permanent was post salvation. After I was saved my heart became transformed from unsettled to restful. The world makes promises but never follows through on those promises. Been there, done that. I was left unfulfilled. Jesus promises that He is the source of peace, and as we walk with Him—He delivers! I have peace from Jesus that is permanent and everlasting.

Let the peace of Jesus flood your heart and fill your mind. Stop trying to find peace in places other than the Lord. When you attempt to get peace from this life, your heart will be troubled and tumultuous. When you focus on God first, your heart will be settled, your mind will be at ease, and you will be at complete rest. When you place your life in God's hands, the result will be a calm heart in the midst of a conflicted world. Focus on Jesus. Trust Him. Be secure in Him. Have faith.

DAY 3

GOD'S PROTECTION

When you pass through the waters, I will be with you; and through the rivers, they shall not overflow you. When you walk through the fire, you shall not be burned, nor shall the flame scorch you. (Isaiah 43:2)

Trials are a constant in life and storms are inevitable. Hardships are going to happen, but you don't have to let the tough times take you down. To have faith through the fire is to find comfort in your Creator even in the middle of afflictions. You can be encouraged even through the onslaught of unexpected circumstances. God is with you!

We are either traveling into a trial, going through a trail, or exiting a trial. This truth would be bleak and depressing were it not for this verse that is chock-full of hope. In this passage God does not say *if* you have trials; He says, "When you pass through the waters," and "When you walk through the fire." Trials will come, but with the Lord we will always be triumphant. It is a comfort to know God is with us wherever we go, including through the fire of affliction. We are not cowardly victims in this fight for the faith. We fight from the place of victory, not from the place of despair.

> The war is won but we will still face little battles on a regular basis.

Through every moment of what may seem like chaos, the Lord consistently upholds us and makes His presence known to us. Our circumstances may not bring comfort to our hearts through hard times, but God's presence will.

As the disciples were on the Sea of Galilee, a violent storm brought fear to their hearts. Jesus was in the boat sleeping. I am certain Jesus would have slept through the storm were it not for the anxiety of His followers. They frantically awoke Jesus, saying, "Lord, save us! We are perishing!" And He arose and spoke a word, causing the storm to cease.

Notice, even with Jesus in the boat the storm still intensely raged. Jesus' demeanor in the midst of the storm demonstrated that God had the whole tempest under control. God doesn't worry about us when we face what we see as incredibly hard predicaments. He doesn't fret because He knows we are His!

The problem is that we sometimes forget this truth when we are in those deep, dark valleys. Circumstances seems to darken and loom over us and we seem to get momentary amnesia. In other words, we lose sight of the fact that God is our shelter, our strong tower and our strength through the storms of life! When we remember the heart of God, we will worry less. When we forget the heart of God, we will be nervous wrecks. Remember that the Lord Jesus is with you on every rough road that you travel on. God isn't going to abandon you because you lack faith. So have faith that God has all things under control.

Know that if God is at peace in your situation, you can be at peace in your situation. He is at rest through the rough times and so you can let fear float away. Be encouraged that your God has you in His hands and will not let you go. It is your job to let go of the control that you think you have and fully lean upon God who props you up and encourages your heart. Trust that the fire of affliction will not burn you, rather it will refine you. The waters will not pummel you; they will purify you! Be encouraged and believe that God's got you!

DAY 4

TRUE LOVE

Behold what manner of love the Father has bestowed on us, that we should be called children of God! Therefore the world does not know us, because it did not know Him. (1 John 3:1)

The Father's love is incredibly overwhelming. To think about how God views His children is one of the most encouraging things in the world. God is love and we are the object of His affection. The Father meets us with open arms and is pleased to spend time with us. May you constantly be aware that the Lord's love is the only true love in this world.

The word *bestow* speaks of both the measure and manner of God's love; it means "one-sided giving." So no matter who you are or what you've done, God lavishes love upon you. "What if I screw up, miss the mark, or temporarily go astray? Won't God abandon me at that point?" Nope. He will run to you, embrace you, forgive you, and give you another chance. After all, God's mercy is never-ending and His grace is forever available.

There is no one on this earth or in this universe who can give you even a small portion of the love that God gives you. Humanity was created because of the love of God! It's important to remember that the Father's love is not dependent upon our perfection; it is unconditional and completely available.

God's love outmatches everyone and everything.

Much of the world does not know or understand our relationship with the Lord. It doesn't make sense to them because it seems too good to be true! When we began walking with the Lord, we realized it is true. The reality is that we can have a relationship with God because He desires a relationship with us. This is such a deep comfort!

I am blessed that God's love doesn't just rain down from above and stops when it hits my heart. It hits our hearts then flows through us so we can share God's amazing love to all, believers and unbelievers alike. Instead of being selfish with His love, we can reflect His love to everyone that crosses our path. His love will neither run dry nor be depleted. May we answer the world's hate with the love of the Lord and may God's love be lifted high for all to see and receive.

Behold and embrace God's love. Revel in His love. Allow yourself to be overwhelmed by His love. The Lord's love is towering, exalted, elevated, extraordinary, and is limitlessly available to you. When you are feeling down, weary, depleted or rejected, remember the deep love that the Father has for you. You are a child of God. You have a Father who wants to spend as much time with you as you are willing to give Him. You are accepted as God's child and are supremely loved. Receive the Father's love and relay His love to others. Allow yourself to be consumed and overwhelmed by the way the Lord views you. God's love overshadows and overpowers all other loves.

DAY 5

TRUE RICHES

My God shall supply all your need according to His riches in glory by Christ Jesus. (Philippians 4:19)

God is your ultimate source of supply. He is your provider, not just in your present circumstances but in your every situation. As you follow Him, you can depend on Him to meet your needs. You may not have an overflow of material goods, but spiritually your cup runs over! Your treasure is the Lord and His Word. Do not live to accumulate material riches; rather, be kingdom-minded and live to build your treasure in heaven.

When the church in Philippi provided for the apostle Paul, he gave God the praise. Paul wanted these Christians to know that the true source of his supply is the Lord. Ultimately, as we place God first in our lives, our material needs are provided for (Matthew 6:33). In those times when we worry about how the bills will be paid or how we will get through another month, we must stay in prayer and in God's Word to remind ourselves that the Lord will come through for us. We may be down to our last penny, but God will provide. Receiving true blessings have nothing to do with the natural, they have everything to do with the supernatural. Our hearts should overflow with thankfulness knowing who is behind every blessing that we receive.

Our Redeemer is the One who makes us rich in this life. We are blessed because of the spiritual bounty that we have in Christ Jesus. The richest people I know are some of the most miserable people I know. I love what Jesus said in Luke 12:34, "For where your treasure is, there your heart will be also."

As we live this life and follow the lead of Jesus, we will clearly see where our true treasure is. Think about the ministry of Jesus. Oftentimes He had no place to stay, He had no food; once He had to borrow money to teach a parable. Jesus' ministry didn't include trying to accumulate as many material riches as He could in order to be content. One could have all the riches in the world and still be empty and depressed. We must remember and realize that true treasure is found in our blessings from above. We are blessed right now.

We are not called to find our security in material things; we are called to find our security in Jesus.

Know that God will supply your every need materially and spiritually. Don't spend your whole life striving to accumulate as much as you can. Don't confuse your needs with your wants, nor fool yourself into believing that you'll be happier and more secure if you have a bunch of stuff collected in your home. Your security and your true treasure come from heaven and not from this earth. Your treasure does not stem from what you see but is the result of what is unseen. Your treasure is poured upon you from above because God loves you. What a blessing.

DAY 6

THE CREATOR'S COMFORT

Blessed be the God and Father of our Lord Jesus Christ, the Father of mercies and God of all comfort. (2 Corinthians 1:3)

Your comfort comes from the Creator of the universe. If that's not mind-blowing, then I don't know what is! The God who made the heavens and the earth is the same One who is with you in and through your hardships. The same God who made the sky and the waters is the same God who gives you shelter from the storm.

The same Lord who spoke the galaxies into existence is the same Lord who brings peace and rest to our hearts.

The God who made it all thinks of us individually. Whether you face intense problems, excruciating pain, or dire difficulties, please remember that the Lord will provide every ounce of comfort you need to get through! God hears you. God's holding you. God will help you. The Lord wants to comfort you because He absolutely loves you. God loves you as if you were the only one on this earth whom He loves! Every day we have a choice to try and find rest in this world or seek His abundant and authentic comfort. When we act as if God were limited in what He can do, our problems will seem enormous. When we view God as the Lord of the impossible, our hardships will seem small and manageable. May our mindset be that God is all-powerful and truly loving.

Sometimes our difficulties seem bigger than human encouragement can cure. When we search for true comfort in everything else except the Lord, we will be left conflicted, depressed and defeated. People cannot completely comfort us like our God can. When sailing through the rough waters of life, we must remember that the Lord is with us *on the boat, at rest.* Many times I forget that God has every one of my situations under control and I begin to freak out a little bit. I attempt to figure things out and try to work things out apart from my God. I'm quickly reminded that my God is with me on the mountaintop in praise as well as in the valley of precarious predicaments. God is with us even when it seems like everything is going wrong and out of control. Permanent peace comes from above. We must look to the Lord for solace because He is the God of *all* comfort.

Your problems are small in comparison to the power of God! You may be going through a difficult place right now and it may seem like the trials will never end! You may not know how long the hardship will last but you can know for sure that the Lord is with you every single step of the way. The shelter that God will give you through the biggest, darkest storm is enough to cover and protect you.

Take comfort that the Creator cares about you so much that He will never abandon you. I encourage you to take a moment and thank God for His presence in your life through it all.

DAY 7

THE GRACE OF GOD

So now, brethren, I commend you to God and to the word of His grace, which is able to build you up and give you an inheritance among all those who are sanctified. (Acts 20:32)

God's grace is greater than your sin. As you walk with God, you have a clear glimpse of the Lord's beautiful heart and amazing attributes. God has given you undeserved spiritual blessings. You didn't earn God's favor nor worked hard to be saved. It's because of His grace that you are built up, equipped and sanctified in this life.

As we get into His Word, we see that God gives His children a plethora of second chances. We are saved by His grace through faith, but His grace extends even further beyond that. If our hearts are willing to receive God's grace, our lives will forever be changed. God's grace will fill every area of our lives bringing the realization that we are blessed and forgiven. God's amazing grace has the capability to destroy any guilt that we harbor and any self-condemnation that we cling onto. Out of love, the Lord lavishes His grace upon all who receive Him and live for Him. God knows that we are failures and that we fumble with mistakes. That reality doesn't stop Him from saving us, setting us apart for Himself and using us in this life. Even with repeated failures the Lord has filled us with faith and loves us as if we had never sinned.

Sometimes it is difficult for me to accept the fact that God loves and forgives me in spite of what I've done in the past. The relieving truth is that He is a forgiver to those who have missed the mark—you, me, and all of humanity. Have an open heart, open hands, and open eyes to see the work God wants to accomplish through you by way of His grace.

> Do not let self-condemnation cause you to sit on the sidelines of God's will.

It's because of His grace that we are driven to deliver His love to this lost and broken world. When heavenly grace is integrated into our lives, it will flow out of our lives and overflow into the lives of others. God's grace is most effective when it is received and then reflected to people who have the exact opposite preconception of what the Lord's heart is like. Many people think that God is a dictator-like leader who is full of nothing but wrath. They believe He is just sitting up in heaven waiting to judge and condemn anyone who is not perfect. They beat themselves up feeling like they are past the point of being forgiven.

I grieve because many churches actually teach this nonsense and create an unhealthy view about who God truly is! We must stick to the Scriptures in order to have the correct view of our amazing and grace-filled God!

As you reach out with the grace of God to people who are struggling, His grace will pull them out of that self-inflicted rut and set them upon the Rock. Be a conduit of God's grace and make sure you are reflecting the heart of God biblically. May the grace of God build you up and everyone who crosses your path!

DAY 8

FORGIVEN

I, even I, am He who blots out your transgressions for My own sake; and I will not remember your sins. (Isaiah 43:25)

When you turn from your sin, you will be forgiven. It's that simple. You don't have to strive to be set free and you don't have to work hard to be forgiven. You don't have to do good deeds to make up for the bad that you've done in the past. When you come to Jesus with true sorrow over your sins, you are forgiven. God will not interrogate you or torture you—He will simply forgive you at that moment.

When we come to the Lord with a humble heart and genuine repentance, God is pleased, and we are forgiven! We are all innately born into sin and fall short of the standard that is set by God. He knows we will make mistakes and falter in the faith. None of us is perfect but as we follow Jesus, we are being made perfect.

I am not where I was nor am I where I want to be as a Christian. One thing is for sure, I continue to move forward in the faith and progress in the things of God. In other words, the Lord is refining me and chipping off those rough edges that are out of synch with Him. I am so blessed that God does not give up on me after I have failed over the same sin. The Lord doesn't bring up my past failures to throw in my face. He doesn't bring up what He's already put behind Him.

In the Gospels Jesus makes it clear that when it comes to serious reoccurring sins, we must go to the extreme to cut them off. I believe the Lord wants us to run to Him with all our struggles so that He can equip us and give us all we need to live a life pleasing to Him. As we are constantly honest with God, He is faithful to forgive us. Forgiveness from the Lord really does result in a freedom that annihilates any guilt in our hearts and lives.

Knowing that God forgives us is not an excuse to perpetually mess up. God works on those weak areas of our lives and constantly gives us the strength and wisdom to break through those sins that hold us back. The beautiful truth is that God wants to grow us, refine us and build us up in our walk. The mark of a mature Christian is not perfection; it is being quick to repent. If we become too comfortable in our sin, it can lead to complacency and compromise. We do not want compromise to have any part in our lives.

Repentance leads to a newfound freedom where love intervenes and God's forgiveness is integrated into our lives.

If you let your past sins run through your mind and pervade your life, you'll be left miserable, hopeless and exhausted. This is not how the Lord wants you to live. If you are walking with God, know that you are free and forgiven. Your sins have been nailed to the cross as Jesus took your place in order to grant you forgiveness. Be quick to repent and know that when you do, you'll be instantly forgiven and free of any and all past guilt.

DAY 9

FEAR NOT

---

*Yea, though I walk through the valley of the
shadow of death, I will fear no evil; for You are
with me; Your rod and Your staff, they comfort
me.* (Psalm 23:4)

The shadow of death is not a destination or a dwelling
place. From time to time the shepherd would have
no choice but to lead the sheep through the valley to
travel onward. It was inevitable when there was no
way around a valley at night.

Occasionally in life we have no choice but to walk
through a valley. Things are not easy and we must
walk on the road of God's will even though it looks
dim and sketchy. The good news is that God is with
us through the valley and He will lead us out of that
valley.

We can walk with ease and comfort because God is
with us. Please don't doubt this truth!

**Seasons in our lives constantly change but we
must remember that God is our constant refuge
and strength.**

In the face of evil, we have no need to fear. Because
the Father places a hedge of protection around us,
we can proceed on God's path with total assurance.
God gives us the supernatural comfort we need to
be at rest in our hearts through every rough road.

He gives us contentment, or peaceful ease of mind, through uncertain times.

Let God's presence wash your worry away and annihilate anxiety that stems from seemingly impossible situations. Be comforted knowing that God is with you, leading you in this life. When you find your comfort in the Lord, no dark valley will ever bring fear to your heart. You are safe and secure as the Father is with you wherever you go.

As you journey through this life, remember to let your Good Shepherd lead you. Let Him go before you so you can have continual comfort in your heart even through those moments that seem difficult. Evil, darkness, and defeat cannot touch you as long as you are following Him who knows the way home. God is with you through the dark valley seasons and He is with you through the sunny days. Rest in that truth!

DAY 10

UNIQUELY CREATED

This people I have formed for Myself; they shall declare My praise. (Isaiah 43:21)

The Lord beautifully formed us, provides for us, and takes care of us. Our hearts are overwhelmingly encouraged as we ponder this truth—we are here because of God's heart. No person is an accident or a mistake. We were created to cry out to our almighty God! We were crafted to call upon the Lord, giving Him every ounce of credit for every blessing we receive. We are God's workmanship; we are His song. We exist because of the Lord's love. Praise Him for this wonderful truth!

> **The result of knowing God's love should be an outflow of praise and adoration.**

We are here on this earth to declare God's praises. When we give glory to the Lord, we are responding to the One who knitted us in the womb. When we praise God, we acknowledge His power and preeminence, and we surrender to His authority in worship and reverence. We yield to His power in an outward expression of adoration and awe.

When I think on the Lord I become awestruck, amazed, and at times, speechless. I love God because when I began reading the Bible, it dawned on me that God absolutely loves me, and it radically changed my life. Not only did God create me because of His love, He works on my heart and helps me to grow and be refined. God made me with a unique personality that's one of a kind and He is molding and shaping me into the man He desires me to be.

God created you and sustains you out of love. Embrace that. Be secure in that. Make it your aim to direct all the accolades to your magnificent God. Respond to the Creator by raising your hearts, hands, and lives to Him.

DAY 11

GOD'S WONDERFUL WORD

All Scripture is given by inspiration of God, and is profitable for doctrine, for reproof, for correction, for instruction in righteousness. (2 Timothy 3:16)

The Bible is beautiful and the Scriptures are stunning. God's precepts are profound and His Word is wonderful. Every book, chapter, verse and word will speak to you as you prayerfully read the God-breathed Word! Jesus said in Luke 11:28, "More than that, blessed are those who hear the word of God and keep it!" By consistently getting into the Scriptures you will be blessed in more ways than one!

God's Word gives the directions that we need for everyday life. We need wisdom for the many decisions we must make every single day. I don't want to take a big step in life without seeking God through prayer and His Word. It can be overwhelming when we blindly attempt to navigate through this life without a roadmap. God's Word is our roadmap, our compass and our blueprint. The Bible is not a book full of questions; it is God's Word full of answers. Not only does the Bible give us direction for life; it also builds up our faith in Jesus.

One significant result of getting into the Scriptures regularly is spiritual growth. I don't want to be stagnant in my faith. I want to remain teachable and forge ahead in my walk, progressing toward godliness and not regressing toward carnality. When our hearts are open to God's Word, then we are setting ourselves up to hear His voice, gain direction and grow in the faith.

> The Bible is not watered-down, sugarcoated or politically correct. It is very honest with issues that matter and affect our lives.

Reading God's Word can cause us to confront those areas of our lives that involve compromise. The Bible will bring to light where we fall short; while at the same time it will equip us where we're not prepared and strengthen us where we are weak. Bringing conviction and correction, it opens our eyes and leads us to repentance. Hearing and heeding the Word of God results in freedom and clarity. Confusion is quashed when we read the Bible with open eyes and open hearts. In a sense, God's Word operates on those areas of our lives that infect our faith, ridding us of habitual sins that reside in us.

Heed God's Word and let it work in your heart. Allow the Scriptures to wash away any and all compromise. God wants to use your life in mighty ways. Let His Word weave its way into every area of your being so the Lord can work! When you remain willing and surrendered and pliable toward God, He will open your eyes, refine your life, and transform you from the inside out.

DAY 12

GOD IS GOOD

You are good, and do good; teach me Your statutes. (Psalm 119:68)

God isn't temporarily good; He is good all the time! Your relationship with God will shape what people think about the Lord. Are you living as if God is good? Are you smiling through storms and praising God through problems? Or when a trial comes, does your very countenance fall and your heart sink? You are blessed to reflect God's goodness to those around you.

If God is good, why do bad things happen? This question has bothered people for centuries and it still nags at many hearts and stops people from following God today.

When people see evil on this earth, God becomes the scapegoat. People shun God and choose not to believe in a deity that would allow such things. They see the sins of humanity and become bitter and angry. We have to remind people that we are in a fallen world and everything is in a state of decay. Every human being is born into sin. Man has free will to either follow the Lord and His ways or not believe and follow their own hearts. Our hearts are innately wicked and unless we repent, get right with God and follow Him, we will do all kinds of wicked and evil actions.

God is good nonstop, and He wants to use you to reflect His goodness to others. We are blessed to be imitators of the Lord so as to demonstrate the heart behind true hope and love. God's goodness is a craving waiting to be satisfied and a beautiful picture of who God is. When we gaze at God's goodness through His Word, we realize why He is good. He is good because, despite our despicable hearts, He loves us. In spite of our shortcomings and failures, He's right there with us.

> When one looks to humanity they will see darkness, but when one looks to God they will see that He is good!

Yes, there will always be evil in the world for the god of this world (the devil) is on a mission to mess everything up and he never takes a day off! Our great calling is to get people's eyes off of life's circumstances that are a result of sin, and instead get their eyes upon the One who is the remedy to sin: Jesus. Instead of looking at the evil in the world and blaming God, we must acknowledge that there is evil but that is what Jesus died and defeated the grave for. He died and rose again to save souls, give hope, and be an example of God's goodness.

In this world that grows dim with time, be a light for the Lord by reflecting His goodness. You don't have to be perfect to be a representative for the Lord and share the gospel, you just have to lead people to the perfect One. We are simply sinners showing other depraved people where to find true fulfillment and purpose. Apart from God there is no goodness, but with the Lord, there is an unlimited supply! God is good all the time.

A CLEAN HEART

Create in me a clean heart, O God, and renew a steadfast spirit within me. (Psalm 51:10)

God can make your convoluted heart completely clean and purify you from the inside out. You just have to be willing and open to the Lord's cleansing up the filth that you've let pile onto your life! Maybe you need to be forgiven and renewed today. Know that the Lord can make that happen in your life. God wants to do a work in you!

As believers our desire must be to come clean with the Lord and allow His forgiveness to saturate our humanness. There's no reason to ever put anything past God because from His perspective, nothing is impossible. You may believe that the Lord would never forgive you for a past failure, but you're wrong. There is no sin too grave that God cannot forgive. The one and only sin that cannot be forgiven is the flat-out rejection of Jesus before a person dies. All other sins can be forgiven when we come to the Lord with a repentant heart.

This prayer in Psalm 51:10 is not sugarcoated; the psalmist acknowledges that he's not perfect. He comes to the Lord in desperation and authenticity. We can and should do the same for God desires to forgive and wipe away every ounce of worldliness that has taken residence in our lives! I don't want to walk around acting like everything is fine when I know I need to repent of an attitude or action that is not of God!

Be real with your Redeemer for He can do a great work in hearts that are greatly willing.

Sometimes we deceive ourselves into thinking that sin has permanently stained us. Although there are real consequences for sin, there is also real forgiveness for those who repent! This is a reason to praise the Lord! The fact is that only God can create, clean, and renew our spirit. When our desire is to get right with the Lord, He is there to begin the amazing process of renewal. Our lives as believers is not a one-time prayer but a lifelong process. God wants to renew hearts and transform lives. As we yield to God, He works, prunes, and refines things in our lives.

Draw near to your Creator and let Him create in you a clean heart. When you are willing to let God purify your heart, you will see and experience profound progress in the faith that God has blessed you with. Your faith will go from dormant to active. Open your heart and let Him do His work of renewal. God can change you and give you a steadfast spirit; you'll be firm in your faith and unwavering in following Jesus. Amazing!

BE TEACHABLE

So shall My word be that goes forth from My mouth; it shall not return to Me void, but it shall accomplish what I please, and it shall prosper in the thing for which I sent it. (Isaiah 55:11)

Reading the Bible will have powerful results in your life. The Word of God can work intensely on your heart as long as you remain open, teachable and receptive. When you have a desire to heed God's Word, you open your heart to receive both correction and comfort. As you remain open to instruction, you'll thrive and flourish in the faith. The Scriptures can speak to you and fulfill the purposes in your life that God wants fulfilled.

When God's Word goes out, many things are accomplished—a seed may be planted, a soul is saved, a heart healed, a relationship restored. It's radical! As we walk by faith we should be continually progressing in the promises of God.

We can be sure that when God's Word goes out to hearts that are receptive, the results will be powerful and life-changing!

Every day you have a choice to open your ears to God's voice or close off communication with your Creator. He longs to speak a word in season to the very situation that you are in. The Lord desires to accomplish spiritual growth in your walk with Him as you remain open to His correction and His instruction. God's Word will work in your life when your heart is willing, and your mind is open to the truth. By making His Word a priority you are setting yourself up to be spiritually healthy.

I'm a firm believer that the way God has grown me since becoming saved has everything to do with consistently reading and praying in God's Word. I've not only learned knowledge; I've been and am being equipped to live out God's Word through my life. It all starts with the Bible.

Consistently read God's transparent Word and you will be placed in a position to spiritually thrive! When you position yourself under the authority of the Scriptures, then you'll grow in the faith and know what God's will is! Read His Word. Wrap His Word around your heart and experience the blessed results of hearing God's voice. Let His Word into the core of who you are. Let it transform your mind and touch your heart.

Are we willing to remain teachable in the truths of God or do we falsely believe we've somehow reached full maturity in the faith? The strongest, most intellectual and most passionate person in the faith still can learn, grow and flourish in the faith! We don't *ever* reach a point where we know it all, elevating ourselves above others because we are the source of truth now. Never. May we all remain teachable in the truths of God and may we never stop growing until the day we are with the Lord in heaven.

A QUIET LIFE

That you also aspire to lead a quiet life, to mind your own business, and to work with your own hands, as we commanded you. (1 Thessalonians 4:11)

This verse demonstrates how to live this life as one who follows Christ. Don't be a show-off; instead, work hard and press toward the purposes God has for you. To be a Christian is to be a reflection of the Lord—by not being rash, sporadic or obnoxious, for instance. Jesus is your example of how to act, react and respond in this world. Follow His lead.

Aspiring to live a quiet life doesn't mean we are to be antisocial and separate from society. We do need to interact with the world because we want to live out and show people how to foster and further a relationship with the Lord. As we look at the Gospels, we see how Jesus exemplifies living in this world. Jesus was not mean, wrathful, angry, or led by emotions that were out of control. He was meek, gentle, lowly and peaceable. Our Savior didn't intentionally try and disrupt or provoke those He disagreed with. In His conversations Jesus took time with people and didn't set out to debate or prove a point just to be right.

He also worked hard! Jesus did ministry from morning until night, speaking truth, teaching, and furthering the kingdom of God. There is dignity in working hard for what matters in this life. When we give ourselves entirely unto the Lord, we may be tired yet satisfied. We will be exhausted, yet eternally grateful.

As we look at the Gospels we see that Jesus is our prime example of how to live in this world.

Mind your own business means "to not disturb the peace." Jesus makes it clear that we are to be peacemakers (Matthew 5:9). Yes, we are to put the interest of others above our own, but we are also to focus on our own spiritual walk. We are to be lights by simply living lives that are purposeful and peaceful. To live a life that reflects peace means to look to the Lord for our calling and to seek to live out that calling.

God uses people to encourage us along the way, but ultimately the calling that we have is between us and God. Don't get caught up in the crowd and just go with the flow of what is trendy today. Instead, seek the Lord and pursue His plans for you! It's not about self-promotion or trying to be known in this world that grows darker by the day. It is about getting your marching orders from the Lord and obeying so as to make an eternal impact in this world. That's what it means to live for what matters.

You are not called to cause chaos, get into a debate, or disrupt someone's peace. Let God lead you to live a life of outpouring love—a life so full of the peace of God that it pleases Him and causes people to see that light shining out of you. You can be a witness by reflecting the heart and life of Jesus Christ, as He commands.

BE A GIVER

I have shown you in every way, by laboring like this, that you must support the weak. And remember the words of the Lord Jesus, that He said, "It is more blessed to give than to receive." (Acts 20:35)

This life is not about you. This life is about you worshiping God and reaching out to others. You were not made to take, take, take—you were made to take in what God has given you and then give it out. Pour yourself out for the Lord and give out what God has given you. Hold on to material things lightly and be careful not to place value on what God does not place value on.

Our natural inclination is to receive rather than to give. We are a culture of constant consumerism and we love our stuff! This is part of the reason so many people are completely miserable in this life. They're always buying new things hoping that they'll finally feel like they have enough. At the end of the day, they are left unfulfilled. We are not living this life to amass as many material goods as we can. We are here to be givers, not takers.

Selflessness means being consumed with God and desiring to receive from Him so we may give to others.

God set selflessness as an earmark of eternal living. Many times we receive, and it stops there. If God has given you a verse that spoke to you, the Lord may give you an opportunity to share it with someone else. If God has given you resources above and beyond, the Lord may call you to give some to a person in need. The blessings shouldn't stop with us. They should flow through us so we can be conduits of what God has given us.

Give an ear to those who need to share their struggles. Give prayer to those who are weak and downtrodden. Give your attention to those who are alone, down and depressed. Give the truth to those who are searching for something genuine and real. Give love to those who are lost. To give is the way to receive blessings from the Lord. The world is all about taking and being ungrateful and unthankful. After all, you deserve it, right? Wrong.

God has given us mercy which means we are *NOT* given what we deserve, which is death, darkness and destruction. We are sinners. Yet, God still loves us, saved us and blesses us. Therefore, every good thing that God gives us is a complete blessing! Give out what God's given you.

Have an open-handed perspective in this life. Don't hold onto useless things with an iron grip. Search for those to whom you can reach out and bless. Rather than having a "mine" mentality, reach out and extend your heart and hands to those who are weak and in need. Like Jesus, reach out and give of what God has given you.

A REASONABLE RESPONSE

Oh, magnify the LORD with me, and let us exalt His name together. (Psalm 34:3)

When we put God in His rightful place, then the result will be praise. He is perfect in all that He does and He will never lead us astray. I find comfort in the fact that God knows exactly what He is doing and He knows exactly where we need to go. God has the answers and as He leads us, we have absolutely no need to worry but every reason to worship.

God is worthy of your praise! He has blessed you tremendously and worship is your apt response. When you respond to Him in awe and amazement, you please the Lord. There are countless reasons to raise your hands and your heart to the Lord, giving Him credit and adoration. God gets us through the most intense trials and the darkest storms. When we focus on His faithfulness, our faith will grow and flourish. Knowing what the Lord has done in our lives should help us realize that He deserves every single ounce of praise that we can possibly give! There are millions of reasons to praise the Lord for He is good!

As we walk with God we will see Him as the God who is limitless and can do the impossible.

Worshiping and being alone with God is intimate and worshiping together with other believers is enriching.

Something powerful takes place as we collectively stand in awe of our amazing God who works in amazing ways! I love being part of a body of believers who respond to the Lord in absolute praise unashamed and uninhibited!

Worship is not a twenty-minute time before the Word of God is preached. It is the reasonable response of a heart that's been touched by the heavenly Father. It is a sweet smelling aroma to the Lord when His people praises His holy name, worships Him for what He's done, and exalts Him for who He is. He deserves all the credit, all the praise and all the adoration we can give.

May your response to God's hand in your life be to fall at His feet in gratefulness. Hold high the name of Jesus. Exalt, magnify, praise and worship your powerful and amazing God. He is worthy to be praised!

DAY 18

ALL THINGS ARE POSSIBLE

Jesus said to him, "If you can believe, all things are possible to him who believes." (Mark 9:23)

You have an overabundance of reasons to fully believe in God. He has worked in and through your life in many circumstances, situations and storms. You may have faced seemingly impossible situations but then God intervened and came through in great ways. As you see the Lord radically work in your life, your faith will continue to increase.

Wholehearted faith pleases the Father; faith opens the door to see the miraculous. But doubt will destroy what God has built up in your life. When doubt creeps in, we may ask questions and inquire about the truth. It is not wrong to be curious and inquisitive. As we go to God's Word for the answers, we will get the answers that will reassure us in God's absolute truth. The result will be stronger, active faith. Another thing that strengthens our faith is when we see God do extraordinary feats in our lives. When we believe God to do the miraculous, our faith will reach the next level. When we walk by faith, we'll witness God do some mind-blowing and amazing miracles that will solidify our belief! All things are possible with God!

This isn't to say that our faith is founded on air and we aren't sure of anything, yet we believe. That's nonsense, of course! To believe in the truth of God's Word and what He has done is to be absolutely sure that His plans will come to pass. There are no recorded promises of God that have been broken.

> Living by faith means knowing that all things are possible with God.

Our faith isn't founded on assumptions; our faith is founded on truth. When we live with this assurance, then our eyes will be wide open to the supernatural and spiritual aspects of life! How we believe stems from what we are looking toward. Look up first. When we adhere to this directional encouragement, possibilities that were hidden are revealed. God will reveal His personal plans for us when we look to Him. Though it may at times seem illogical, God is beyond logic. He can shatter our preconceptions of impossible things. God can transform a huge obstacle into something that is feasible and possible!

When your perspective includes God's promises, your faith will soar and be solidified. He can do what you think He cannot do. Don't put anything past the Lord. Believe. With your whole heart, believe. May you focus on God so steadfastly that your faith becomes unstoppable. You know that God can do anything; now is the time for you to start living like it!

DAY 19

COMPLETE FREEDOM

Therefore if the Son makes you free, you shall be free indeed. (John 8:36)

Faith in Jesus results in complete freedom—freedom from the prison called "the world" and "the flesh." To be bound is to allow anything and anyone other than the Lord lead your life. You don't have to fall into the devices of the devil any longer. When you accept and walk with Jesus, you are absolutely free!

Freedom stems from Jesus dying on the cross. He said, "It is finished." The work has been done and the price has been paid to get us out of darkness. We are not free because we did a really good job at being spiritual. The Lord Jesus took the punishment that we deserved. If we just surrender and lay our lives upon the finished work of Jesus Christ, we are set free.

> We can breathe a sigh of relief knowing that Jesus was nailed to the cross so that our sins would no longer imprison us.

Jesus not only breaks our bondage to sin; He frees us from every ounce of burden in our lives. If we feel like the weight of the world is upon us, we must let the Lord into every facet of our hearts. Adhering to a life of faith means living in such a way that no chains could ever restrict us. Nothing could ever stop us from getting the gospel out in this dark and dreary world!

Freedom means looking to the Father's plans instead of our own surface level dreams. Freedom means finding joy in Jesus even when our circumstances seem to be nothing but negative. Freedom means falling face first at the feet of Jesus Christ in humble submission and complete adoration. Surrender leads to complete liberty in the Lord. What an astonishing and comforting blessing!

Today is the day to fully give your life to Christ and fully live for Him! Jesus loves you so much it's almost unreal! Yet, the reality is that Jesus died for you personally. He took your sins upon the cross and you are free because Jesus did the work for you—but you still need to remember to daily surrender to Him. Your Christian walk will be radical when you truly grasp that you are completely free in Christ. Nothing can hold you back. Jesus has already handled it. Praise Him!

DAY 20

WONDERFULLY MADE

I will praise You, for I am fearfully and wonderfully made; marvelous are Your works, and that my soul knows very well. (Psalm 139:14)

You are unique and one of a kind. Never try to be someone else because God created you with a personality that is pleasing to Him. God loves and values you like a doting Father does with His beautiful child. You were made to connect with people with the personality that He has blessed you with. Embrace that. Be secure in that. Believe that.

Our aim should never be to emulate another person so much that we try and be them.

When I was newly teaching the Bible, I would attempt to be like the pastors I looked up to. It came across forced and it just wasn't me. I quickly realized that I needed to surrender that desire to the Lord and be who God created me to be. When I did, then God began using me to a greater degree.

Yet, the Lord loves us so much He refines our hearts and creates in us a passion to live for Him. Spiritual growth is an essential part of the Christian life and the Lord wants to see us bear fruit for Him! God will work on our hearts to grow us and conform us to His image.

Philippians 1:6 says, "Being confident of this very thing, that He who has begun a good work in you will complete it until the day of Jesus Christ."

> God created you and is crafting you into who He wants you to be.

God's works are astonishing and out-of-this-world wonderful! As we marvel at our surroundings, we can thank God for all His hand has made—including us! This is not a prideful or conceited outlook at all. The Lord framed us out of love. When a person works on a project or builds something, he values that finished product because he is happy with it. We are God's workmanship and He created us to make a difference in this dark world. We can thank God for knitting us in the womb and sustaining us through this life. We can thank God for every breath and every day that we have life. We can thank God that He uses us for the purpose of furthering His kingdom. How marvelous are His works!

DAY 21

DON'T GIVE UP

I press toward the goal for the prize of the upward call of God in Christ Jesus. (Philippians 3:14)

Don't stop. Don't give up. Don't give in. Keep pressing forward and plowing through the dirt called the world. It may be tough at times, but you will get through because God is with you. The easy thing to do is quit and give up; to believe the discouragement from people who don't share your God-given goals. The reality is that you were created to run for the Lord Jesus. Keep your eyes upon Him as you head toward your divine goals!

God gives you every ounce of strength you need to navigate through every terrain and season of life. Therefore, you can run your race of faith with confidence and press on for eternity. The Lord has a purpose and plan for us—a heavenly goal that we get to live out and follow through on. We are literally alive to live out the purposes God has for us. That's mind-blowing! We are not called to live for superficial things, nor are we called to get stuck in the minutiae of life. We are called to boldly live for what matters!

We live for more than what we can see, feel and hear.

We are not ever called to let our feelings direct us in this life. Our emotions fluctuate and our opinions often change, but the truth of God always remain the same! We are to get God's truth out to as many people as we possibly can in order to further the kingdom of God. What a blessing and privilege we have as Christians!

Sometimes we lose sight of our goals and abandon our resolutions. However, there is one goal that we cannot afford to neglect. That goal is to give glory to God. That is our calling that stems from heaven. When we are serving the Lord Jesus and working toward heavenly treasure, rather than building an earthy kingdom on this earth, we are fulfilled. Earthly kingdoms don't last; they don't stand and they will not remain. If it were not enough that we'd be with Jesus for eternity, He also promises us rewards!

Serving God with the right heart is never in vain. When you pour your life out for your loving Lord, passionate to make Him known, you will be so blessed. Always remember that you are called to focus your love, attention and affection upon Him. Press on toward the goals God has set for your individual life and don't look back! Enjoy running your race of faith and find joy in going all for God's plan for you.

DAY 22

GOD'S PROTECTION

You have also given me the shield of Your salvation; Your right hand has held me up, Your gentleness has made me great. (Psalm 18:35)

God protects you and places an unseen shield around you. The opposition may be harsh, but our God is gentle. The Lord shields you in ways that you do not even know about. You can assuredly rely on Him to be triumphant in every area of your life. Part of God's provision is His protection from spiritual enemies and spiritual darkness. You can confidently know that the Lord will take you down His path and keep you safe along the way.

Spiritual battles go on all around us constantly. The enemy and his followers are attempting to tear away our faith and fill us with doubt and unbelief. Those moments when we are discouraged or feel down and out for no reason are not from the Lord. They're from the enemy who works overtime to try and undo all that God has done and discredit all that God is doing now!

Yet even with all the opposition coming against us, we have no reason to worry or fear! The Lord has us and nothing can snatch us out of His hands (John 10:28). Worries are easily washed away at the realization that God is with us wherever we go and whatever we do. Therefore, there's no reason to fret and worry. Our salvation is secure, we are set apart for the Lord and we are shielded from the enemy and his workers. What a comfort!

God gives peace to our hearts as His presence brings protection.

The Lord is capable of being our strong defender, giving us the weapons to withstand the tactics of the enemy. He will pave a way through the biggest mountain of discouragement and clear a path on the roughest road. Knowing this should give us godly confidence to keep on taking steps of faith daily.

The Lord also deals gently with us, with an abundance of grace and mercy. His right hand holds us up when we are weary and weak. God is our strength through the storm, our clarity through conflict, and our wisdom through the worst circumstances. Be blessed to know that God fights for us and extends His love in a gentle, loving way. The Lord's love is real and it never runs dry. Your heart is in God's hands. Trust Him with it. Live fully for Him knowing you have been set apart to live for what truly matters in this life. Nothing can steal you away from the Lord and no one can take away your salvation. His strong hands will never let you go.

PEACE FROM GOD

Let the peace of God rule in your hearts, to which also you were called in one body; and be thankful. (Colossians 3:15)

God is the source of peace and the solution to hardships. Sometimes we don't live like we are experiencing God's peace. Instead, we stress out, we worry and we overthink everything resulting in a very anxious mind and unsettled heart! People wonder what's wrong with us and why we are so stressed out. These moments are a wake-up call indicating that we are not trusting in the Lord and we are not seeking Him for peace. We strive in our own strength and attempt to do it all ourselves. If you want serenity, the source of peace is the Savior in your heart.

Don't let turmoil tear apart your heart. Don't let stress steal away your joy. Don't let anxiety annihilate your happiness. Let God replace your problems with His peace! When you let the peace of God rule in your heart, the result will be overwhelming joy! Relief truly is the result of letting God's peace fill your heart and give you rest in your soul.

If we let the world's chaos dictate our state of mind, we'll be weary. Exhaustion doesn't come from the Lord; it comes from us trying to live apart from the Lord. When our hearts lean toward the Lord, we will experience overflowing rest! Peace comes from the Lord above who rains down His peace into our hearts.

> Serenity comes from resting in the Father's love instead of settling into the world's way of living.

People strive and work their whole lives in an attempt to gain happiness someday. Without the Lord that day will never come! The day true peace resides in our hearts is the day we start walking with the Lord! Rest is never the result of working really hard—it comes from God ruling in our heart. On the other hand, ruin is the result of letting the world run your heart. So the question becomes, who are you going to let rule your heart—God or the world? I don't want to strive or be stressed out all the time. I want to surrender to the Lord and rest in Him through it all. When you let God into every facet of your heart, you will have His overarching and overflowing peace. Jesus will settle your heart and calm your mind.

DAY 24

UNABASHED WORSHIP

Then David danced before the LORD with all his might; and David was wearing a linen ephod.
(2 Samuel 6:14)

When you demonstrate genuine worship and heartfelt praise, it pleases the almighty God. You are unashamed to raise your hands, heart and life to the Lord. As you worship God, you are responding to the countless ways He has worked in your life. Do not let anything hinder your praising Him!

When the ark of God was being returned to Jerusalem, David was so joyful that his immediate response was to dance unabashedly in public. He expressed himself as a result of a blessing that was taking place.

It is good to joyfully respond to the Lord in adoration and praise. Do not hold back when you worship Him. The joy of knowing God and the blessing of obedience to Him is enough to overflow your cup. Worship God with a genuine heart that heralds the truths of the Lord. You were made to worship. You were created to respond to the Lord in praise for all that He has done and all that He will do in your life!

When we begin each day saying, "Here I am, Lord," we surrender our plans to God and replace them with His plans. The natural realm is the top layer of life;

the supernatural realm is what we must truly live for. To see the spiritual realm of life, we come to the Lord in prayer, praise and obedience. Obedience leads to an outpouring of deep worship.

Built in our hearts from birth is an insatiable need to respond to the Redeemer of humankind. Joy comes as we focus on and respond to Jesus! As believers, we should be both realists and optimists. Realists because we believe in the truth that is contained in God's Word, and optimists because God leads us, loves us and blesses us!

Pessimism has no place in the Christian life. We're not called to be Eeyores walking around with our head low and our countenance glum. God didn't create us to see only the negative all the time and never realize God's blessings. We are called to be Tiggers! To be excited about what God is doing, to have true hope, and to recognize and respond to the awesome work that the Lord is doing!

> Instead of looking in, looking back or looking ahead, look up!

Seek God and see His hand upon your life. Let go of inhibitions and let God see and hear praises flowing from your life. The least we can do is respond to the Lord in worship that is real, genuine and from our hearts to His. Be awestruck at your awesome God and let your heart truly awaken to all He has for you.

DAY 25

AWESOME THINGS

He is your praise, and He is your God, who has done for you these great and awesome things which your eyes have seen. (Deuteronomy 10:21)

God has done a work in your heart and life and He continues to work in indescribable ways that are above logic and beyond your understanding. The response from your heart toward His should be intense awe! As you follow the Lord, what results is an action-packed adventure lasting for the rest of your time here on earth!

Epic actions and feats come from our amazing God! Every plan God enacts in our lives is a life-changing, awe-inspiring plan. The fact that we get to be in the middle of God's mission for us is nothing short of astounding! As we stay in God's perfect will, we will not only see the natural, we'll see the supernatural at work. Those spiritual things that Jesus was always trying to direct people's eyes toward will be revealed to us. We aren't called to live for surface level things, we are called to go deeper and see things through the eyes of faith! We praise the Lord because He is praiseworthy in every way! We see God's greatness in the works that He achieves and the purposes that He promotes. As we continue to walk with the Lord, He continues to blow us away with the way He leads us, manifesting His miracles along the way. We can't help but to personally praise our God because He is the object of our worship!

What amazing feats have you seen God do in your life? Think about it. Make a list even. Contemplate how the Lord always comes through and how His plans never fall through. Maybe He has worked in your life in some mind-blowing ways that have left you speechless. Maybe He has accomplished His purposes through you, even when you have felt like you weren't going to get through another day! The more in tune you are with the Lord, the more you will see God's marvelous miracles.

> Our faith is not based on hoping things would happen, our faith is based on the great things God has done in our lives!

When we ponder the "great and awesome things that our eyes have seen," the result will be a heart of gratefulness and a life of surrender. We are blessed! Let us not neglect to praise God for His fulfilled promises. He has come through for us time and time again. Be in awe of His amazing works and worship the One who does a multitude of miracles. Give all the glory, honor and praise to the One who does beautiful and unexplainable things in our lives. He is more than worthy.

DAY 26

LET FEAR FALL

The LORD is on my side; I will not fear. What can man do to me? (Psalm 118:6)

God fights for you and He is on your side. As a result of your connection with the Father through Jesus, fear should not be on the radar of your mind. Fear can be placed aside, forgotten, forsaken. Do not let daily situations in life cause anxiety to bubble to the surface and crowd out faith from your heart. Allow fear to fall, leave it on the ground, and walk away.

There are so many irrational fears that people fight against and allow to defeat them. Fears will not only sidetrack us, they can actually weaken the solid faith that God has built within us. Where once faith has awakened, fear will knock it out! Statistically, most of the things we fear never come to fruition. In other words, those things that we often worry about are hypothetical and may never come to pass. It's time to abandon those irrational *what if* questions and live in reality. A true follower of Jesus will let their fears be crushed forever.

Fear leads to a vicious cycle of inactivity for the kingdom of God. The calling that God has given begins to seem irrational, out of our reach and impossible to live out. Faith is powerful enough to kill your fears! Your alliance with God will remove all earthly fears and wash away your worry, down the mountain into the inhabitable abyss that we will never visit. God makes fear go away in an instant when our faith is activated daily!

> When our faith is active, defeat will shift from a reality to a silly concept that could never happen.

People may intimidate you and evoke fear in you. What can they really do to you that would strip away your faith? Nothing as long as you remain equipped and ready for whatever comes your way. The Bible says to be ready in season and out of season (2 Timothy 4:2). As we stay in God's Word, consistently pray and continue to have fellowship with like-minded believers, we will be spiritually ready for anything!

Eternal matters are the real substance of this life. No one can touch your faith in God. The Lord has saved and sealed you. He has you in His hands. Therefore, people can do no harm to the areas in your heart that truly matter. You never have to let others dictate your attitude and emotional state. Fear is from looking inward, outward and downward. Faith is a result to looking upward to the Lord who has filled you with faith. Now it's time to willingly allow the Holy Spirit to activate that faith and live how you were meant to live.

Remember that God is with you and on your side. When you live a surrendered life, you will never be fighting against the Lord. Do not let the enemy stunt your spiritual growth by allowing fear to lead your life. As you progress on God's path for you, make sure to forsake fear and never let it dictate your decisions. You are right where God wants you. The Lord loves you, forgives you and gives you security in Him.

DAY 27

HIGHER WAYS

For as the heavens are higher than the earth, so are My ways higher than your ways, and My thoughts than your thoughts. (Isaiah 55:9)

Our plans may fall through the cracks and lead to a multitude of problems, but God's plans are always perfect. His ways are the right way for us to go. God's Word, the Creator's love letter to us, is what clarifies His plan and keeps us on the road of His will.

The Scriptures set us on a path to fulfill God's purposes: first we get saved, then we come to know Him, and then we walk on the path He has planned out for us. This is what the Christian life is all about! There are times where we have no clue what God is doing or where He is leading. The Lord is sovereign over our circumstances and He knows exactly what He is doing! At times we attempt to take control of our own life. We quickly realize that God knows best. His thoughts and ways are way higher than our thoughts and ways. May we never get to the point where we usurp the Lord's authority and try to be the captain of our own destiny. When we try to take control of things, we will be out of control and off of the road of God's will. When we live like God is in complete control, we will not be stressed out; we will be free and relieved.

> Even during those unsure and unsettling moments we can fully trust that God is in control.

God is perfect and good. Therefore, as we look to the perfect One to find clarity on our path in life, He will lay out His plan for us. As we seek Him through prayer and His Word, His perfect plan comes into focus. The Lord is our guide and as we submissively follow His lead, we will always be led in the right direction!

One of my pet peeves is when I lose my way driving. I have to seriously pray for patience because I feel out of control since I've no idea where I am. Anxiety can start to creep into my heart and worry starts to invade my mind. But then as I pray to the Lord, He reassures me that He's got me and there's no need to fret! God is a God of reassurance and comfort. Ultimately our plans will leave us lost and full of regret. The Lord's plans will lead us to the destination that He designed for us. Trust Him. Rely on Him. Lean upon Him. Know that He is in total control of your circumstances and situations.

God has a future that's perfect for you and a hope that He wants to work into your heart. His plans for you are good and He always knows where you need to go. All you have to do is get into His Word and He will reveal the course you should travel. When you set your sights on Jesus, you can be sure you'll be right on course. Real wisdom comes from the Lord and He knows what and where is best for you. Seek Him, trust Him, and see what adventures He lays out for you!

DAY 28

TRUST HIM

Those who know Your name will put their trust in You; for You, LORD, have not forsaken those who seek You. (Psalm 9:10)

You can trust God and depend on Him every day and in every situation. The Lord is a promise keeper and He's always 100 percent dependable. Leaning on the Lord will bring a rest to your heart and a relief to your mind because you are casting your cares upon God who is happy to take those stressful burdens away!

Trusting the Lord means yielding to Him in every area of your life. As a result of depending upon God, you will sense His presence and see His promises come to pass.

I am seriously astounded at how God has worked out difficult situations in my life as I just stayed faithful to Him in the small things. We struggle when we don't stay consistent in trusting the Lord. God is the One who holds things together and He will always be there for us. We know His name and we know what He's capable of because He has a perfect track record. When we trust in faulty human beings for what only God can do, we will be let down and we will fall down in helplessness.

When we don't fully trust God, it is like saying we pick and choose when we depend upon Him and when we depend upon ourselves. The problem with this is we don't even know our own hearts! How can we trust in ourselves when we are faulty sinners? We can't! There is only One God whom we can totally depend upon in this life!

> Every day we have a choice to trust in people or in the Provider.

You can trust in human imperfection or in God's perfect promises. The Lord will never let you down. Not only will God keep His promises, He will never leave you—ever. With people we have definite doubts. With God we can be 100 percent sure all of the time.

Make sure your trust in God does not waver. Know that He is with you; those promises He's given you will come to pass. If God has given you a clear promise, hide it in your heart and pray for supernatural patience. If it is from Him, it will happen. God is with you as you seek Him in complete dependence.

DAY 29

WISDOM AND DIRECTION

If any of you lacks wisdom, let him ask of God, who gives to all liberally and without reproach, and it will be given to him. (James 1:5)

God wants you to ask Him for wisdom to navigate through this life. You have doubted and you have been unsure about many decisions that you've had to make. When you have no clue what to do, ask the Lord for wisdom! God always knows what to do, which way you should go, and what decisions you should make. The Lord will not get mad at you for constantly asking for wisdom and direction. He welcomes your prayers and answers your petitions.

We all need wisdom. We make countless decisions every single day. One wrong decision can lead down a path that is far from God's perfect will. When we integrate God's wisdom into our world, we can know that we're walking in God's mission for us. There is only one source of true wisdom—God! He gifts us with all the wisdom we will ever need from day to day.

There have been times where I was unsure about what to do in a situation. I tried everything to attempt to make the right choice, but to no avail. As a last-ditch effort, I sought the Lord for wisdom. As a result, the Lord led me to make the right decision which got me onto the correct path. It was a reminder to me that God has all the answers to stay in the center of His will.

When wisdom shines down from above, we will have godly confidence in every single decision we must make.

Without the Lord we would be lost and adrift. Walking without wisdom will leave us lost, empty and alone. Thank God for the wisdom that He showers upon us and for the blessings He lavishes on us from above! God will give us more wisdom than we know what to do with. He will never be put off or annoyed by us asking for wisdom on a regular basis. He welcomes our communication with Him!

Know that when you ask God for wisdom, He will give it liberally. You are not called to figure life out all on your own. God knows what He's doing and He knows where you need to go. When you ask God for direction, you will not be disappointed; you will be directed onto the right path and you'll make the right decisions. Wisdom is integrated into your life when you simply ask your almighty God to fill you with wisdom.

DAY 30

THE ONE WHO GOES WITH YOU

Be strong and of good courage, do not fear nor be afraid of them; for the LORD your God, He is the One who goes with you. He will not leave you nor forsake you. (Deuteronomy 31:6)

When you are connected to the Creator, fear will be far behind you. As you consistently walk with God, His presence will be transparently with you and you'll have strong faith. Skepticism will drown in the deepest part of the sea as you are reminded that God is always present and He will never abandon you! Knowing God goes with you wherever you go will give you complete confidence in and through all your endeavors and adventures. When you are conscious of God's presence with you, peace, strength and courage will be the result.

Courage comes from the Creator, so let fear go and cling to the Lord. Opposition may come against us and attempt to bring us down, but God has our back! He is there for us to defend us, to fight for us and to protect us. There is no need to worry and every reason to worship! Wherever we go and whatever we do, the Lord God is with us. Sometimes we forget that the presence of God is with us and we start to worry and stress. As we get into His Word, as we seek Him through prayer, and as we stay connected with strong, like-minded believers, we will be built up, assured and confident in Him! Without God in our lives we have absolutely no strength or endurance. Yet, when we are weak is when the Lord's strength is made evident in our very lives.

> Oftentimes opposition is actually an opportunity to cling to the One who is our strength!

I think that sometimes we underestimate the Lord's power and we forget that He is capable of anything! He is God and we are not! When we plug a device to an outlet, power will flow from the source; and the same is true with the Lord. He is and always will be our source of power! We're not called to conjure up power from within ourselves, nor are we called to lean upon others for empowering. The only real power in and out of this world is the power of God! As we draw near to Him, His power will propel us to be more courageous, more bold and stronger than we've ever been.

Be courageous. Stay strong. Let go of fear. When you realize God's presence is with you, it will integrate strength, courage and boldness into your life. God is good. He always has been, and He always will be. The more connected you are to Him, the more power you have to live a life that is purposeful. The Lord will never leave you because He loves you. God wants to use you in this life! He is waiting for you to call upon Him. Today is the day.

CONCLUSION

When you focus on God your faith will grow. You'll have control over distractions that threaten to pull you away from the things of God! If you just "let things happen," then you will focus on everything else except for eternal things! We must be intentional when it comes to our active walk with God.

There have been times where I've lost sight of what matters in life and the result was confusion, fear and purposeless living. I understand that many people get distracted and lose focus easily. Admittedly, I'm one of those people! Yet, the more I seek God and implement healthy spiritual habits into my life, the more I grow and the more I desire to focus on things above. Before you get out of bed and your feet hit the floor, seek the Lord in prayer and open up His Word. Let exploring on your phone always come after seeking God first.

When I focus on God first, I am reminded what life is truly about. We are here to build the kingdom of God and let people know they don't have to remain lost and depressed. We are here to make an eternal impact and give hope to the hopeless and help to the helpless. Let's focus on God first and let the things of God consume us to such an extent that people are influenced by our eternal outlook!

Made in the USA
Middletown, DE
15 May 2022

65786996R00044